HERE'S WHERE HISTORY HAPPENED!

GETTYSBURG

BY JANEY LEVY

Gareth Stevens
PUBLISHING

Please visit our website, www.garethstevens.com. For a free color catalog of all our high-quality books, call toll free 1-800-542-2595 or fax 1-877-542-2596.

Library of Congress Cataloging-in-Publication Data

Names: Levy, Janey, author.
Title: Gettysburg / Janey Levy.
Description: [Buffalo, New York] : Gareth Stevens Publishing, [2025] | Series: Here's where history happened! | Includes bibliographical references and index. | Audience: Grades 2-3
Identifiers: LCCN 2023053425 (print) | LCCN 2023053426 (ebook) | ISBN 9781482466355 (library binding) | ISBN 9781482466348 (paperback) | ISBN 9781482466362 (ebook)
Subjects: LCSH: Gettysburg, Battle of, Gettysburg, Pa., 1863–Juvenile literature. | Gettysburg (Pa.)–History–Juvenile literature.
Classification: LCC E475.53 .L54 2025 (print) | LCC E475.53 (ebook) | DDC 973.7/349–dc23/eng/20231205
LC record available at https://lccn.loc.gov/2023053425
LC ebook record available at https://lccn.loc.gov/2023053426

Published in 2025 by
Gareth Stevens Publishing
2544 Clinton Street
Buffalo, NY 14224

Designer: Tanya Dellaccio Keeney
Editor: Theresa Emminizer

Photo credits: Cover Jon Bilous/Shutterstock.com; series background pixelparticle/Shutterstock.com; p. 5 Peter Hermes Furian/Shutterstock.com; pp. 6, 11 (top), 19 (top) Everett Collection/Shutterstock.com; pp. 7, 9, 17 (top) Courtesy of the Library of Congress; p. 11 (bottom) Christopher Heaney/Shutterstock.com; p. 13 benoitb/iStock.com; p. 14 Janusz Pienkowski/Shutterstock.com; p. 15 https://upload.wikimedia.org/wikipedia/commons/1/10/Lincolnatgettysburg.jpg; p. 17 (bottom) Andy Sutherland/Shutterstock.com; p. 19 (bottom) https://upload.wikimedia.org/wikipedia/commons/9/9b/Gettysburg_Address_Bliss_copy.jpg; p. 21 Daniela Collins/Shutterstock.com.

Printed in the United States of America

CPSIA compliance information: Batch #CSGS25: For further information contact Gareth Stevens at 1-800-542-2595.

CONTENTS

Words in the glossary appear in **bold** type the first time they are used in the text.

HAVE YOU HEARD OF GETTYSBURG?

Have you ever heard of Gettysburg? It's a small town in southern Pennsylvania with a population of about 8,500. But even though it's small, it occupies a huge place in U.S. history.

Two important events happened at Gettysburg. One was a big battle fought during the Civil War. The other was a famous speech given by President Abraham Lincoln called the Gettysburg Address. You'll find out about both events in this book.

KNOW THE FACTS!

GETTYSBURG WAS FOUNDED IN 1786. IT WAS NAMED AFTER SAMUEL GETTYS, WHO WAS AN EARLY SETTLER AND OWNER OF A PUB.

WHAT WAS THE CIVIL WAR?

In the Civil War (1861–1865), Northern states and Southern states fought each other over enslaving people. Southern states' **economy** was based on enslaved labor on farms. Northern states opposed enslavement. Their economy was based on factories and railroads, not enslaved people.

Abraham Lincoln, who opposed enslavement, was elected president in 1860. Southern states feared he would end enslavement. So 11 Southern states withdrew from the United States and formed a country called the Confederate States of America. And war started.

KNOW THE FACTS!

PEOPLE WERE BROUGHT BY FORCE FROM AFRICA TO BE ENSLAVED ON SOUTHERN U.S. FARMS. AT THE START OF THE CIVIL WAR, THERE WERE ABOUT 4 MILLION ENSLAVED PEOPLE IN THE U.S.

COTTON WAS THE MOST IMPORTANT CROP OF THE SOUTH, AND GROWING COTTON WAS HARD WORK. ENSLAVED PEOPLE HAD TO CLEAR THE LAND, PLANT THE SEEDS, CARE FOR THE PLANTS AS THEY GREW, THEN PICK THE COTTON WHEN IT WAS READY.

THE BATTLE OF GETTYSBURG

You might think a battle lasts a few hours. But the Battle of Gettysburg lasted three days, from July 1 to 3, 1863! Major General George Meade led about 94,000 Union, or Northern, soldiers. General Robert E. Lee led about 72,000 Confederate, or Southern, soldiers.

The battle started at Cashtown. However, all the Union soldiers hadn't arrived, and the Union had to withdraw to Gettysburg to escape the larger Confederate army. It wasn't a good start. But when the battle ended, the Union had won.

THIS PICTURE, WHICH WAS MADE IN 1887, SHOWS AN ARTIST'S IDEA OF WHAT THE BATTLE OF GETTYSBURG WAS LIKE.

KNOW THE FACTS!

GENERAL LEE'S CONFEDERATE SOLDIERS HAD WON ANOTHER BIG BATTLE RIGHT BEFORE GETTYSBURG. HE HOPED THAT IF HE WON THIS BATTLE, THE SOUTH WOULD WIN THE WAR.

A TURNING POINT

The Battle of Gettysburg is considered a turning point in the Civil War. That's because the Union army stopped the Confederate army from **invading** the North and forced it to turn back to the South.

General Lee had thought the Confederate army could win this battle. He believed winning the battle would bring the war to an end. And the Confederate States of America would then be a free country, separate from the United States. The Union win ended these dreams.

KNOW THE FACTS!

IF LEE'S CONFEDERATE ARMY HAD WON AT GETTYSBURG, IT WOULD HAVE BEEN IN A POSITION TO ATTACK IMPORTANT NORTHERN CITIES SUCH AS PHILADELPHIA, PENNSYLVANIA; BALTIMORE, MARYLAND; AND EVEN WASHINGTON, DC!

THE MASON-DIXON LINE WAS AN UNOFFICIAL BORDER BETWEEN THE NORTH AND SOUTH DURING THE CIVIL WAR. GETTYSBURG WAS IMPORTANT FOR THE CONFEDERATES BECAUSE WINNING THERE WOULD HAVE MEANT THEY SUCCESSFULLY INVADED THE NORTH.

THE BLOODIEST BATTLE

Although the Union won the Battle of Gettysburg, the cost was terrible. Gettysburg was the bloodiest battle of the Civil War. The total number of **casualties** was around 50,000. That equals the population of a small city!

The Union side had 23,055 casualties: 3,155 killed, 14,531 wounded, and 5,369 captured or missing. It's harder to give exact numbers for the Confederate side. But guesses are that there were almost 5,000 killed, almost 13,000 wounded, and almost 6,000 captured or missing.

THIS PICTURE SHOWS THE TERRIBLE FIGHTING OF PICKETT'S CHARGE.

KNOW THE FACTS!

PICKETT'S CHARGE, ON THE LAST DAY OF THE BATTLE, IS FAMOUS FOR HOW HORRIBLE IT WAS. GENERAL LEE SENT BRIGADIER GENERAL GEORGE PICKETT'S TROOPS TO ATTACK THE UNION, LEADING TO ABOUT 6,000 CONFEDERATE CASUALTIES.

TO HONOR THE DEAD

Part of the Gettysburg battlefield was turned into a new cemetery, or graveyard, for the Union soldiers who died there. A special event was held on November 19, 1863, to mark the cemetery's opening.

Edward Everett, one of the most famous speakers of the day, was invited to speak at the event. President Lincoln was invited to make a few brief statements. Everett spoke for two hours; no one remembers his speech today. Lincoln spoke for about two minutes. His speech is famous.

EDWARD EVERETT

KNOW THE FACTS!

FIVE WOMEN FOUGHT IN THE BATTLE OF GETTYSBURG, AND AT LEAST ONE DIED THERE. AT LEAST 250 WOMEN DRESSED AS MEN AND FOUGHT ON BOTH SIDES DURING THE CIVIL WAR.

THIS PICTURE WAS TAKEN AT THE EVENT WHERE LINCOLN GAVE HIS FAMOUS GETTYSBURG ADDRESS.

LINCOLN'S MESSAGE AT GETTYSBURG

In his speech, President Lincoln wanted to make sure people understood why soldiers were fighting and dying, not just at Gettysburg but at all Civil War battlefields. To accomplish his purpose, he connected the Battle of Gettysburg to history.

President Lincoln talked about the ideas of liberty and the equality of all men stated in our nation's **Declaration of Independence**. He warned that if the Union lost the war, our form of government might disappear.

THIS IS ANOTHER PICTURE TAKEN THE DAY LINCOLN GAVE THE GETTYSBURG ADDRESS, SHOWING THE HUGE CROWD GATHERED FOR THE EVENT.

KNOW THE FACTS!

IT'S A **MYTH** THAT LINCOLN WROTE HIS SPEECH WHILE ON THE TRAIN TO GETTYSBURG. HE LIKELY WROTE PART OF IT BEFORE LEAVING THE WHITE HOUSE ON NOVEMBER 18 AND THE REST THAT EVENING.

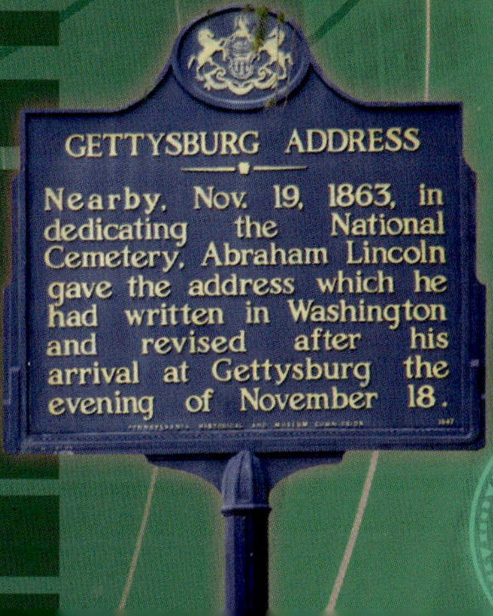

WORDS FROM THE GETTYSBURG ADDRESS

"Four **score** and seven years ago our fathers brought forth on this continent a new nation, **conceived** in Liberty, and **dedicated** to the **proposition** that all men are created equal. . . .

It is rather for us to be here dedicated to the great task remaining before us . . . that this nation, under God, shall have a new birth of freedom—and that government of the people, by the people, for the people, shall not **perish** from the earth."

THIS IS A PRINTED COPY OF LINCOLN'S GETTYSBURG ADDRESS.

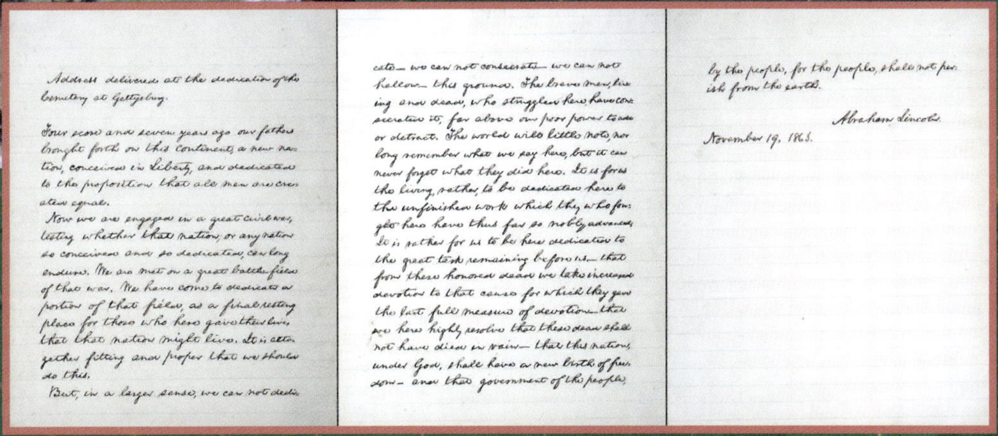

Address delivered at the dedication of the
Cemetery at Gettysburg.

Four score and seven years ago our fathers
brought forth on this continent, a new na-
tion, conceived in Liberty, and dedicated
to the proposition that all men are cre-
ated equal.

Now we are engaged in a great civil war,
testing whether that nation, or any nation
so conceived and so dedicated, can long
endure. We are met on a great battle-field
of that war. We have come to dedicate a
portion of that field, as a final resting
place for those who here gave their lives,
that that nation might live. It is alto-
gether fitting and proper that we should
do this.

But, in a larger sense, we can not dedi-
cate— we can not consecrate— we can not
hallow— this ground. The brave men, liv-
ing and dead, who struggled here, have con-
secrated it, far above our poor power to add
or detract. The world will little note, nor
long remember what we say here, but it can
never forget what they did here. It is for us
the living, rather, to be dedicated here to
the unfinished work which they who fou-
ght here have thus far so nobly advanced.
It is rather for us to be here dedicated to
the great task remaining before us— that
from these honored dead we take increased
devotion to that cause for which they gave
the last full measure of devotion— that
we here highly resolve that these dead shall
not have died in vain— that this nation,
under God, shall have a new birth of free-
dom— and that government of the people,
by the people, for the people, shall not per-
ish from the earth.

Abraham Lincoln.

November 19, 1863.

KNOW THE FACTS!

THE GETTYSBURG ADDRESS TALKS ABOUT "A NEW BIRTH OF FREEDOM." THIS MEANT THE END OF ENSLAVEMENT AND FREEDOM FOR ENSLAVED PEOPLE.

GETTYSBURG TODAY

Did you know you can visit the place where the Battle of Gettysburg took place? You can, and almost 1 million people visit each year.

When you go there, you can tour the battlefield with a guide. You can visit the cemetery where Union soldiers are buried. There's also a **museum**, where you can see objects from the war and listen to accounts of the battle written by people who were there. You can discover so much more about Gettysburg by visiting!

EVERY YEAR, PEOPLE GATHER AT GETTYSBURG TO REENACT, OR ACT OUT AGAIN, THE BATTLE. IF YOU GO AT THE RIGHT TIME, YOU CAN SEE IT!

KNOW THE FACTS!

AT GETTYSBURG, YOU CAN ALSO VISIT THE DAVID WILLS HOUSE. THAT'S WHERE PRESIDENT LINCOLN STAYED THE NIGHT BEFORE HE GAVE THE GETTYSBURG ADDRESS!

GLOSSARY

casualty: Someone who has been hurt, killed, captured, or gone missing.

conceive: To invent, or to bring into being.

Declaration of Independence: The piece of writing in which the colonies said they were free from British rule.

dedicate: To open to public use.

economy: The money made in an area and how it is made.

invade: To enter a place to take it over.

museum: A building in which things of interest are displayed.

myth: An idea or story that many people believe but that isn't true.

perish: To come to an end.

proposition: An idea or suggestion.

score: A group of 20 things or people.

FOR MORE INFORMATION

Books

Hubbard, Martha. *Gettysburg*. Lake Elmo, MN: Focus Readers, 2024.

Yomtov, Nel. *Abraham Lincoln and the Gettysburg Address: Separating Fact from Fiction*. North Mankato, MN: Capstone, 2021.

Websites

The Battle of Gettysburg
https://kids.nationalgeographic.com/history/article/gettysburg
Learn more about the Battle of Gettysburg and see some great pictures on this website.

The Gettysburg Address
www.abrahamlincolnonline.org/lincoln/speeches/gettysburg.html
Find out more about the Gettysburg Address and read the words in the five known copies of Lincoln's most famous speech.

INDEX